Henry Wilder Foote

In Memory of Charles Sumner

Sermon preached at King's Chapel, Sunday, March 22, 1874

Henry Wilder Foote

In Memory of Charles Sumner
Sermon preached at King's Chapel, Sunday, March 22, 1874

ISBN/EAN: 9783744755146

Printed in Europe, USA, Canada, Australia, Japan

Cover: Foto ©Lupo / pixelio.de

More available books at **www.hansebooks.com**

IN MEMORY OF CHARLES SUMNER.

SERMON

PREACHED AT

KING'S CHAPEL,

SUNDAY, MARCH 22, 1874.

By HENRY W. FOOTE.

AND

SERVICES AT THE FUNERAL,

MARCH 16, 1874.

PRINTED BY REQUEST OF THE WARDENS AND VESTRY.

BOSTON:
ALFRED MUDGE & SON, PRINTERS,
34 SCHOOL STREET.
1874.

SERMON.

"Righteousness exalteth a nation: but sin is a reproach to any people."

"For, behold, the Lord, the Lord of hosts, doth take away from Jerusalem and from Judah the stay and the staff, the whole stay of bread and the whole stay of water, . . . the honorable man and the counsellor, . . . and the eloquent orator."

"I will make a man more precious than fine gold: even a man than the golden wedge of Ophir." — Prov. xiv : 34 ; Is. iii : 1, 3 ; xiii : 12.

THE Old Testament might be called the *New Test* (if we cared to play upon words), — the most modern touchstone to which we can bring character and duty, public or private. There are those, indeed, who deem it to be obsolete because it is old, — a method of reasoning which would banish the light of the solar system from the universe, nay, which would abolish the universe itself as utterly antediluvian. But the fathers of New England knew the rock on which they builded, when they strove to found their commonwealth on the eternal principles which they read on the ancient tables of stone ; and the living waters of conscience and duty which have quickened the souls of their children, which are the hope of the republic to-day, have flowed forth from those granitic summits of immemorial law, as the stream gushed forth from the rock which Moses smote.

There are those, too, who sometimes deem that religion belongs in a region apart from the strifes and questions of political life. And this is partly true. Religion is at home on the Mount of Transfiguration, above the smoke of the camp-fires and the noise of conflicts, where the heaven is nearer; but she does not take men up with her there unless she meets them in the plain, where in the dust and heat of conflict she is a light on their way and an inspiration in their spirit. We should all agree that questions of the day should not be made a *religion* of; that the church is no place for criminations or discords. But religion should be made a *question of the day*, — every day. And since she should be the most vital factor in every personal duty, and since no duty is more personal to every man and woman, under a system of government like ours, than that which concerns the public weal, it follows that the church has sometimes the necessity laid upon it of trying to show how religion bears on public duty and public service. And here, again, the Old Testament fairly blazes with light. It may almost be termed the great Manual of Political Duty; and we

need ask no better test of its inspired power to mould
humanity towards the ideal future than is afforded by
comparing its starry words, glowing in the firmament
of truth with the light of justice and freedom, with the
wisest maxims of the masters in statecraft, from Ma-
chiavelli's Prince and the Testament of Peter the Great
of Russia, to the Bismarckian theory of a diplomacy
gangrened with falsehood, or the idea that a nation is
to be ruled by packing a caucus. When you come to
deal with any question of public morals, or when you
seek for words with which to describe a faithful public
servant, the difficulty is not how to find, but what to
choose, out of the riches of this Old Testament, so New.

Our texts strike the chord to which our thoughts
must perforce attune themselves to-day. A certain
theme is laid down for us by the proud duty which fell
to this church of being the voice of this dear old
Commonwealth of Massachusetts in her public service
of mourning for one who had served her so long in
the highest office in her gift. I could not, if I would,
put aside the task which seems to be written for me in
the signs of public mourning which still remain on
these walls.

The part which this church took in those solemn of-
fices was due, as you know. not to our basing any claim
upon the former connection of Senator Sumner with

this church, but to our placing the church at the service of the State government for the rites of honor which it sought to render; and these dark drapings still hang here, in sympathy with the legislative vote which retains them at the Capitol during the period of public mourning, because we were a part of the State and acted for the State. Yet there was a special fitness — a sort of family right — in our association in those memorable services when the streets of the city were like the aisles of a crowded church, and this house of prayer was as a central chapel. For many years of his life were rooted in this church; his father was its clerk during a part of the Senator's childhood; his mother I knew well, as her pastor, in the gentle loveliness of an old age, subdued by the chastening of many and singular sorrows;* and we have a right to think that probably the clarion call of the Gospel wrought within him, more than he was himself aware, from the Christian teaching of those faithful men and lovers of truth and righteousness whose names are our heritage and our inspiration. † Yet I do not propose to make this the occasion for a Commemorative Discourse of Eulogy: such a discourse will be given elsewhere, and by one qualified to speak, — as the legislature may determine. Much has been already said by

* See Note A, appended.

distinguished men in public places, and the time for
Congressional Eulogy is still to come. My duty here
is other than that, — very simple, yet very true. It is,
to try to impress on ourselves, while the feeling of the
hour is fresh, some of the principles which we need
more than ever to insist on in our judgments of public duty and our actions as faithful citizens. I would
say nothing to open old feuds or strifes, now forever
silenced; nor is it needful to stir the embers of that fire
of controversy which consumed the nation for so long,
— now happily turned to ashes and as far back of us
as the flood. I pray that no word of mine may bring
us down from the high level of a common sympathy, in
which, as at great moments of our war, the whole heart
of this Commonwealth has been melted into one.

There is, indeed, something sublime in the healing
and reconciling work which is wrought by death. Out
of that silence comes to us a deeper lesson than all the
voices of life have ever been able to bring home to us.

> "That which the open book could never teach
> The closed one whispers."

We feel this when we stand beside the humblest and
poorest clay that has enshrined an immortal spirit. But
how much more when it is one who has been a power
in the land, whose name has been a watchword of pas-

sionate admiration and of intensest opposition, who has been a factor in the history of a tremendous period, not to be left out in the tracing of causes and results! When sudden stillness falls on such a one, and all the tumult of tongues is quieted or turned to a rivalry in praise of things not always so greatly valued while they were with us, how falsely does it seem that we speak of him who brings this to pass as " the king of terrors "! Rather does he seem to come as the angel of peace. And we may well say, with Sir Walter Raleigh, " O eloquent, just, and mighty Death! whom none could advise, thou hast persuaded; what none hath dared, thou hath done; and whom all the world hath flattered, thou only hast cast out of the world and despised. Thou hast drawn together all the far-stretched greatness, all the pride and ambition of man, and covered it all over with these two narrow words, " *Hic jacet.*" Yes! He covers over those things which partook of mortal weakness and infirmity; but the things which are immortal, great memories of great gifts, faithful thoughts of faithfulnesses to conscience, tried experience of long fidelity, — these are not covered, but now first begin to be revealed and fruitful in the fullest sense, as the seeds of a flower fall from the bursting capsule on fertile ground.

There is no higher calling in human society than

that of the public service in a nation of freemen. Ambition in this direction is a worthy ambition.* It is the duty of every man that he should be ready to meet the obligation of such service if it comes to him; we should train our children to this readiness as one of the most imperative duties of manhood. But this ambition may be a lamp to lighten the path of him who walks in it, with lofty purposes, thorough preparations, righteous scorn of every mean and low thing; or it may be a snare and pitfall to his conscience, causing him to stumble in winding and slippery ways, — if he reach the coveted place only dragging down its honor to his own base level. The one is a noble flame, kindling the spirit to climb the hard

" Steep, where Fame's proud temple shines afar,"

And to write one's name high among the benefactors of the human race: the other is the degradation and often the ruin of the nation which it plagues. But as the public service is perhaps the highest, and certainly the most shining, so is it also the most difficult

---

* This is nobly expressed by Mr. Sumner : —

" No true and permanent fame can be founded, except in labors which promote the happiness of mankind."

In "this true and noble Valhalla will be gathered only those who have toiled, each in his vocation, for the welfare of the race. Mankind will remember those only who have remembered mankind." — *Works*, ii ; 32, 41 : Oration on Fame and Glory.

way of duty. I say nothing of the storms of obloquy from foes, or the beclouding influence of flattery from false or unwise friends. These may be hard to endure or to resist; but the arduousness of high responsibility is not here, but in the responsibility itself. For consider what various qualifications — and how impossible to unite in a single person — are demanded to meet all the exigencies of a great place in the councils of a nation. What kind of man should a great people desire to fulfil all the ideal possibilities of high public service? He should be, should he not, a combination of the recluse scholar and of the practical man of affairs; wise with the wisdom of books and with the deeper wisdom of experience in human nature; reading the history of the past as an open page, and learning from it the lessons so easy for a nation to be taught by others' experience, — since all nations are made up of the same human nature, — so costly for a nation to be taught by its own mistakes: reading the characters of men by that trained instinct which cannot be deceived. He should be practised in the school of statesmanship, that highest and most difficult of arts, which consists not in managing men by their low and base motives, for mere party success, but in shaping the policy, whether commercial or moral, of a great nation, with far-seeing perception of the causes that lead to prosperity or to decay. He should be kindled by the ardor of great convic tions of truth and righteousness, ready to face unpop- ularity for the faith that is in him, yet never hasty or unjust; with a calm, deep comprehension of the views most opposed to his own, able to do justice to their convictions, and to find every ground of conciliation and mutual respect. Strong with a commanding personality, and with powers able to compel respectful recognition, he should fulfil that Eastern proverb which says, "A man that knoweth the just value of himself doth not perish," yet should have that re- spect for others' judgment which most surely wins their assent to the influence of a stronger nature, and should be untinged by that self-reference which centres the universe in itself. Eloquent with a manly strain, the power of his persuasion should never be embittered by words of personality or scorn. To borrow a figure from science, the spectrum of his speech should be rich in the rays of light, rather than in those of heat. He should be *before* his time in vision, yet *with* his time in comprehending sympathy; with forward-looking sight, but backward-reaching hand, to lift his people to his level. Must we say, in the republic which Washington founded, in the State which sent the incorruptible Pickering to his counsels in war and peace, and has inscribed the names of John Adams and John Quincy Adams on the roll of his successors, that such a public servant must have an integrity above suspicion, with hands clean from money-getting and from office-seeking,— that he should have a lofty independence and a single eye to the public good ?   We live in a day when these plain dictates of honor and conscience are *distinctions* to be named with praise.   He should be crystal pure from the vices of passion or of meanness, clad in an asbestos robe of principle to walk through the fires of the temptations which beset public life without so much as the smell of smoke upon his garments.   He should sit at the feet of no human master, but he should have sat at the feet of Christ.   The eternal principles of His Gospel of righteousness should glow in his heart, and the wisdom of his law of kindness should pervade his conduct with its fragrant breath, while in the lowly faith of a disciple he should be "as a little child."   Of a public servant so endowed, it may well be said, in the words of the prophet, " I will make a man more precious than fine gold : even a man than the golden wedge of Ophir."

And now, if we look at the distinguished record of that eminent servant of the nation whose finished life is close to our thoughts to-day, — not in the spirit of indiscriminate eulogy, but in the dispassionate attempt to anticipate the judgment of another generation, with that frank independence of judgment which he himself signally illustrated, we shall surely say, Some of these great qualities Senator Sumner had in abounding measure; in others he was lacking. Perhaps no man ever lived so all-sided as to have them all: he who has the greater part of them must stand high in the remembrance of a grateful country, especially when the traits which distinguish him are those which the land needs to brace its conscience and renew the integrity of its will.

It has been the fortune of Mr. Sumner to be associated more intimately than any other public man with the most agitating questions of our time. And this was no accident, but essential in the very nature of the man. From the very beginning, his character was a blending of two sides of character rarely united, — strenuous self-culture, and earnest, if not defiant, championship of the redress of wrongs. I do not need here to retrace the familiar story in detail, or to recapitulate what is in part so well known to his fellow-townsmen, and is in large part written on the history of the country itself. Of the years of study in our Boston schools, at the neighboring University (to which his noble bequest has tes-

tified to his enduring filial affection), in his close
relation of pupil with master with Judge Story, of his
studious years at foreign universities and in London,
at a time when foreign study was comparatively rare,
he might truly have said, in the words of the English
poet whom he loved so well : —

> When I was yet a child, no childish play
> To me was pleasing ; all my mind was set
> Serious to learn and know, and thence to do
> What might be public good ; myself I thought
> Born to that end, born to promote all truth,
> All righteous things. *

He returned here with marked distinction at the
same age at which Milton again wrote to his friend
Diodati, " Do you ask what I am thinking of ?   So
may the good God help me, of immortality." Or it
might have been the words of his own friend, De
Tocqueville, in which he might have said, " Life is
neither a pleasure nor a pain, but a serious business
which it is our duty to carry through and to terminate
with honor." Eleven intervening years were filled
with various labors, — professional, literary, and philanthropic, — which I do not need to enlarge on here.

---

* These lines from " *Milton's Paradise Regained.*" Book I, were placed by the
engraver under Jansen's portrait of Milton, at the age of 10.   See for their
application to the poet's own life, *Rev. J. J. G. Graham's " Autobiography of
John Milton,"* p. 11.   London : Longmans, Green & Co.   1872.

Meantime, the ominous cloud which rose above the hori-
zon with the annexation of Texas spread and darkened
more and more ; the war with Mexico followed ; then
came the dark days of 1850, when a call rang through
the land, parting friend from friend, brother from
brother. The student of history finds in those years
the seeds sown which were harvested in civil war, and
finds that Mr. Sumner was each year more prominent
as one of the voices of the ever-growing conviction
against slavery in New England. He was a little
more than forty years of age, — that stage of life when,
as he once said, " according to a foreign proverb, a man
has given to the world his full measure,"*—when he was
chosen to succeed Mr. Webster in the Senate of the
United States.† The Quaker poet of New England
tells me that at this time he confessed to him that he
had a great ambition, but not for political life, — that
his ambition was to become a jurist, or to write history. In that desire he would have satisfied the needs
of half of his nature, — the contemplative side ; but
the other half, the side of action, could never have
been content without a great field of action and of
power. And what a field it was on which the Senator
from Massachusetts entered in that stormy time! As

---

* *Works*, vi ; 504 : Eulogy of Hon. Goldsmith F. Bailey.
† Mr. Webster's seat, vacated by his becoming Secretary of State, had been
filled for the remainder of his term by Hon. Robert C. Winthrop, during nine
months, and Hon. Robert Rantoul, for a fortnight.

I have stood within the halls of the old senate chamber, plain and bare, which shook with the thunders of Webster's reply to Hayne, or within the palatial new chamber, which saw the working out of the drama of the civic side of the great war for the Union, and the associations of the place have crowded upon me, and I have remembered what echoes those walls would give could they but speak what they had heard, it has seemed to me that no place on earth was such a sphere for worthy action or such a point of leverage for the eloquence which would not end in words, but shape the public will of a nation. Rufus Choate, who knew it well, wrote to Mr. Sumner, " How does the Senate strike you ? The best place this day on earth for reasoned and thoughtful yet stimulant public speech."* " When I think what it requires," wrote Mr. Sumner himself, on his election, " I am obliged to say that its honors are all eclipsed by its duties."† To such a sphere the Senator from Massachusetts came,— one of the youngest of that august body, without experience in public affairs, the bold and outspoken representative of a small minority in Congress and of a growing fire in the North. Ten days ago he was the senior member of the body, trained by twenty-three years of its great duties,— a longer sum of years than

---

* See Mr. Choate's letter, quoted in Mr. Sumner's *Works*, iii ; 2.

Works, ii ; 438: Acceptance of the office of Senator of the United States.

the office had been held by any Massachusetts senator
since the foundation of the republic,— and he had seen
the words, which when he spoke them were deemed
the enthusiasm of a fanatic, surpassed by the stupen-
dous reality of the history through which we have
lived. He might have applied in his own case the
words in which Mr. Mill, in his autobiography. speaks
of some matters in his own parliamentary career:
" My advocacy of" them was "at the time looked
upon by many as personal whims of my own; but the
great progress since made by those opinions,· and
especially the response made from almost all parts of
the kingdom to the demand, fully justified the timeliness
of those movements, and have made what was undertaken as a moral and social duty a personal success."
The fiery heats of those years before the war the next
generation can never know; for the battle which
they will have to fight has but one side,— the fight of
honesty against corruption : while the hardest part of
the struggle which preceded the downfall of slavery was
that men at the North, equally good, equally true.
were on opposite sides, and each could hardly avoid
misjudging the other. " The high contention" is now
" hidden by the little handful of earth"; but in its
record future generations will trace the manifest up-
heaval of the tremendous forces which were to shake

the nation to its foundations. It was the fateful blow struck by a mad hand in answer to words spoken by him in his place as senator which made Mr. Sumner a *symbol* of the Northern idea. From that hour, the silence of his suffering spoke with a louder tongue than his most intense words. Then came the war, when the strife of tongues gave way to the strife of arms; and for ten years, as Chairman of the Senate Committee of Foreign Relations, he filled one of the most important posts in the government so as to win the respect alike of enemies and friends; and then three years of loneliness as ' a voice crying in a desert, Make the crooked straight and the rough places plain '; and the scarred warrior, who had been in the forefront of the battles of his time, passed from storm into rest. He had reached what he himself once called " the grand climacteric, that Cape of Storms in the sea of human existence." *

He was buried with the mighty mourning of a sovereign State, as befitted the first Senator from Massachusetts (with one exception only) † who ever died in office, — the senator who had held office for nearly a generation of incorruptible life, the faithful voice of

---

* *Works*, i; 148: Notice of Judge Story.
† Hon. Isaac C. Bates of Northampton died at Washington, March 16, 1845, and was eulogized by Mr. Webster in the Senate.

liberty and justice. Such is the barest outline of the external history of those tremendous years when "the fountains of the great deep were broken up," and that commanding presence was always where the storm was wildest.

And now, when we ask for the secret of his power, we find it, first, in that which was a weakness as well as a strength, — namely, the strong imperiousness of his convictions. He could not overstate them, they were so pronounced and positive ; nor could he easily deal justly with opponents. Political charity is the rarest of the virtues, — rarer, by a strange law, in proportion to the moral and philanthropic quality of the opinions which one holds. The very fact that conscience and the sense of right are so engaged makes it wellnigh impossible to see how the conscience of honorable and good men may be engaged in adverse views. O hard fate, when the sense of justice to an oppressed race contended with the sense of duty to a bond whose rupture might cause the sun of the Union to go down in blood, and good men among us, both hating the giant wrong, both loving the starry constellation of the States, were sundered by an impassable gulf! It was in the nature of the man who swung what he called "the great Northern hammer" to strike hard and stern blows ; and if in his record are found words which pass

the mutual respect of high debate, or which follow the
method of prophetic denunciation rather than that of
statesmanlike conciliation, we cannot doubt that now,
out of the wisdom of death, he would speak to us to
say that if he could live his life over, he would do some
things differently.

But other men have had convictions as strong and
imperious as his without becoming identified with them
as the acknowledged exponent and representative of
a principle. His strength was in the identity of his
principle with that of New England. He was "a Puritan idealist." In all its differences of form, there lived
in him that most persistent type, which has impressed
its character on the civilization of our whole country,
which was strong enough to subdue granite and ice
and make a home for their children. The Puritans
were impracticable men, — a projectile cast into England, of such tremendous explosive force that when it
burst, the fragments flew across 3,000 miles of ocean.
They were men of a narrow conscience, and like some
strong stream, the deeper and the more resistless in its
flow because of the very narrowness Their indomitable spirit is cast into a word by " Andrew Fletcher,
whose heroical uprightness amid the trials of his time,
has become immortal in the saying, that he ' would read-
ily lose his life to *serve* his country, but would not do a

base thing to *save* it.'"* The children of the Puritans
are still the same; and we, who are of them, can afford
to acknowledge that the fathers would have been sometimes hard to live among, and that there is danger that
even conscience and zeal for righteousness may be at
times obstinate and one-sided. But one thing is certain, — that when these things are in the line of the
ideas of justice, freedom, abstract right, they have irre-
sistible power over the mind of the race which has
grown on our rocky soil. Men who are tempered
with this spirit are better fitted to point a thunderbolt
than to weld a nation; they belong in the time when
controversy has passed beyond compromise. So far
from sympathizing with that rule of practical statesmanship which old Hesiod sings, —

"Half is more than the whole,"

There can be for them nothing less than the ideal whole.
The only rule of yielding or giving up what they know
is in that saying of another Greek, —

"We must sacrifice to Truth alone."

It was the power of the Senator that he voiced this
intense Puritan strain in the ideas of the New England
conscience. Said one of his most ardent friends of

* *Works,* i; 69.

him, in the heat of a political campaign : * He is "patient in labor, untiring in effort, boundless in resources, terribly in earnest, . . . the Stonewall Jackson of the floor of the senate, . . . both ideologists, both horsed on an idea."

Essentially characteristic of this moral intensity, which makes the typical New England character like one of those Iceland geysers, a boiling hot spring in the heart of the glacier, is an elevated confidence in one's own intentions, tending in small natures to self-absorption, but in great natures to utter absorption in a great cause, and giving an assurance of right which could make the Senator choose for the motto to his collected works, the proud appeal with which he would speak to future generations, those words of Leibnitz: "Veniet fortasse aliud tempus, dignius nostro, quo debellatis odiis, veritas triumphabit. Hoc mecum opta, lector, et vale." One who knew and loved him well sums up this characteristic in these words in a letter to me : " He struck for the right and was sure he saw it. He had a sublime confidence in his own moral sagacity, greater than I have ever seen in any man ; and, let me add, events usually justified such confidence." †

* Mr. Wendell Phillips, quoted in *Works*, vii ; 243.

† Rev. J. W. Thompson, D. D.

And this zealous intensity in the man was served by an indomitable power of work, such as has rarely been equalled and probably never surpassed by any one in the public service. I have the testimony of two of his private secretaries to the fact that his strength and fidelity in the unseen labors of his duty as senator, and on the most responsible Committee of Foreign Relations, exceeded anything that can be imagined. He "toiled terribly." The key-note of his life is struck in an early lecture of his on "The Employment of Time," * whose text is the famous exclamation of Titus, "I have lost a day!" and he might well leave as his legacy to those who would profit by his example the words of Seneca: "Vita, si scias uti, longa est." High office was to him no holiday perch, but an opportunity for more strenuous work, nor did anything so chafe him as enforced abstention therefrom. All the wide resources of a various learning were reinforced continually by special preparations, and he carried the student's habit of toil into the position where men are apt to think that they are officially infallible on all questions, from finance and diplomacy to the filling of the pettiest office.

And this is strikingly shown by that monument of labor, yet uncompleted, — the edition of his Works.

* *Works*, i: 184.

As during the recent days I have read through the
seven volumes, I have been impressed with many
things, but with none more than this. From that oration
on " The True Grandeur of Nations," which sounded
again, in such rich and high-wrought strain, the note
which Rufus Choate had struck the year before in the
United States Senate, when he said, " War is the
most ridiculous of blunders, the most tremendous of
crimes, the most comprehensive of evils,"— an idea
emphasized in these words, which form the key-note
of Mr. Sumner's oration : * " War is known as the
Last Reason of Kings. Let it be no reason of our Republic ; " — to his last speech in the senate, there are
the same characteristics, — a labored affluence of illus-
tration from widest sources of study, a style elaborate
even to excess, but, throughout, the sense that here is
one who has made thorough preparation for the great
office of advising the Elders of the Republic.

And one can hardly read these volumes without
a deeper realization how truly the Senator was not
only a prominent figure, but a powerful actor in the
greatest chapter of modern history. Friends will find
nothing save to admire ; old enemies, much to differ
in ; and those who have been independent from personal ties or by-gone discords, both much to admire

* *Works.* i : 110.

and something to regret. But all must agree in
reading the superscription of his name on page after
page of most eventful annals. If Abraham Lincoln
shall stand forth against the black background of the
war as the Cromwell of our great struggle, only far
purer, more unselfish than the Ironside Puritan was,
the name of the persistent friend of emancipation, who
stood to him in wellnigh as close a relation as did his
Latin Secretary to the Protector, will shine in the
same constellation. The future historian will perhaps picture the two in scenes which are already re-
corded,— the Senator taking his French friend with him
to see the morning levee which that kindly heart, all
burdened with presidential cares, yet found time to
give daily to the poor who needed him most,—the sick
soldier or the poor widow,— with the invitation, "Come
with me and see St. Louis under the Oak of Vin-
cennes"; or the President, a week before his martyr-
dom, reading aloud to the Senator. on the deck of the
steamboat that carried them to evacuated Richmond,
those prophetic lines in Macbeth : —

Duncan is in his grave :
After life's fitful fever he sleeps well.
Treason has done his worst : nor steel, nor poison,
Malice domestic, foreign levy, nothing
Can touch him farther !

4

But no future historian will be able to describe in all its dramatic intensity the struggle which involved these men, so different, and the parts of the nation which they represented, — the one eager always for the highest and furthest thing, the other gauging the exact mind of the people with that pre-eminent political sagacity. He will try to describe the one " crying aloud and sparing not," as the voice of the most advanced conscience of the North, the other telling him " You are only ahead of me a month or six weeks,*" — till at last the proclamation seals the policy of the government. He will describe the growth of the institution of slavery on this continent, from the time when the Mayflower, with its cargo of liberty, and the first slave ship, with its cargo of human bondage, were crossing the ocean at the same time in 1620, to the time when, like the genie of Arabian fable, the little cloud, released from the hold of that vessel, darkened all the land, a giant in strength. He will tell, too, how the man who spoke the intensest sentiment of the North was ever urging the principle of absolute liberty, and would venture where it seemed wild to go, as the Douglas who bore the heart of Bruce to the Holy Land threw his sacred trust far before him into the hosts of the infidel, to witness that he would

* *Works,* vi : 152.

never give over his advance; and then he will tell
how the great work was done by the hands of men
differing widely in their sentiment even on the great
question of universal liberty, but agreeing in being
willing to die for their country, — that not the voice
alone of eloquent oratory, but the deeds of devoted
patriotism wrought the marvel of freedom. Let yon
der marble speak,* with its proud record of men who
could be silent and give their lives; to testify how the
great power of the land stood behind the Act of Emancipation, and made it, instead of a bit of paper, a
reality! And then think of those long rows of colored faces, the representatives of four grateful mil-
lions, that on Monday last gleamed with hardly sup-
pressed emotion, as of men parting with a mighty
friend; and remember the coat of arms of Lord Ex-
mouth, on which "was emblazoned a figure never
before known in heraldry,— *a Christian slave holding
aloft the cross, and dropping his broken fetters.*"† Happy, indeed, is he whose name is forever linked with
the eternal ideas of freedom and justice!

The lofty and permanent lesson which remains
with us from the life of Senator Sumner is one pecu-

* The monument " In memory of the young men of King's Chapel who died
for their country, 1861-1865," erected in the church in 1867, records the names o
fourteen who died, out of the nearly sixty sons of the church who engaged in the
war.

† *Works,* i; 463: White Slavery in the Barbary States.

liarly needed in our time,— that of independent loyalty
to the best conscience. Whatever else fails, that cannot fail. Not always does success come; not always
do the wonderful forces of public awakening, the mad
ness of enemies, the awful arbitrament of war, justify
the political seer with the attainment of his vision.
" Prophets and kings have died without the sight.'
But for fame, as well as for one's own inward peace, the
surest warrant is the boldest venture. Trust in the
eternal truths of conscience and duty and God! The
sober wisdom of that homely precept of one of our
great poets, " Hitch your wagon to a star," will be
acknowledged in the end.

Who now remembers, in his dispraise, that John
Milton staked his all on a losing cause, that he was
an extremist and a fanatic, that he spoke hot and bitter
words against the enemies of his party? But that
which shines in him is the pure and lofty spirit, the
consecration of great powers to his country's service
in a time of storm, — putting aside the plans of quiet
study and literary ease, — the great pleadings for
liberty and righteousness, the soul that "was like a
star and dwelt apart."

We learn, by contrast with those things which in the
presence of great death compel our reverence, what

are the dangers of the land. What kind of man is he whose public service will prove the public servitude, and will drag a nation towards its fall? We have already described him by opposites. He will be one educated enough to know the evil side of men, able enough to compel their reluctant help, wise in the secrets of corruption, who has grown rich from the misfortunes of his country, who mounts to power over heaps of blackened reputations, and uses every office but as a round in the ladder of his ambition; who rules by fear, yet whose friendship is even more blasting than his hatred. Detected again and again in wiles which would wreck the good name of better men, he will almost persuade the multitude to believe his shame to be a new form of virtue. If ever such a man should come, woe to the nation which he tricks towards its doom! for then, indeed, " Politics become a game, and principles are the counters which are used." *

But such men would have little power of evil in a country, if there did not exist grave elements of danger in the atmosphere of the time, in those murky dispositions of the public mind to which they act as the lightning-rod on a lowering thunder-cloud, to draw the fatal shock. First among these, we must name the worship of money for money's own sake. So long as

* *Works*, ii ; 154 : Letters on Parties, etc.

men and women believe that this has any worth in
itself, apart from the question *how* it has been won, and
will let foul gains win a fair name, teaching their children by precept to seek above all things to be honest,
and by practice to seek above all things to be rich;
so long as they fear the wholesome frugality of our in-
corrupt ancestors more than they fear dishonor, and
add a double bribe to the temptation to get wealth
in doubtful ways, by respecting it after it is so got;
when the prizes of political preferment are gilded with
unclean perquisites, and leaders high in place sway the
nation through the purse-strings of their base tools and
batten on the spoils of industry; so long as a consid-
erable part of mankind look leniently on Judas, because he carried the bag, we may well be thankful for
one example for lofty integrity, so pure and high that
he could say, " People talk about the corruption of
Washington : I have lived here all these years and
have seen nothing of it,"— so true that no slander dared
sully his reputation with the suspicion of a bribe.

And then there is the worship of power for power's
own sake. Forgetting that ability, apart from moral
gifts, is the sharpest cutting-tool, sure to turn in the
hand that uses it unless it is grasped by firm principle, our people are tempted to idolize the very qualities
by which the angels fell, and in which the chief of

fallen angels is also chief. They count impudence and brazen audacity a sign of power; but do they think what power mere unscrupulousness may give a man? The moment he flings honor and decency to the winds, his power for evil in word and deed is multiplied ten-fold. What then? Shall we straightway make the lack of scruple one of the cardinal virtues, and teach our children to take the "*Not*" out of the ten commandments? Or shall we turn again to the reassuring thought of a man of state who could hold high office for nearly a generation; whose motto was those words of Story, "No man ever stands in the way of another"; * whom, having held such office, none accuse of turning it into an engine for private advantage ; who sought sincerely to make the ends he aimed at in it his "country's, God's, and truth's "; who believed himself the servant, not the master, of the Common wealth, whose honors sought him, and were un marketed as they were unbought?

And yet again we are in danger of disbelief in the honor of the honorable. In the hot and heavy fumes of accusation and of proven failure to do clear duty which befog the air, when great names are tarnished and honors well earned are cheaply lost, the tempter whispers that it is so the world over,—" There is none

* *Works*, i : 147 : Tribute to the late Judge Story.

upright; no, not one." Who shall measure the inspiration which there is in such an hour in the unspotted example of a great integrity towering above the mean rivalries and small ambitions of petty greatness as a rocky New England summit towers over the surrounding plain?

And if we are tempted to be discouraged, seeing a wide distrust of educated skill; that the community is prone to think that statecraft comes by nature or in flattering the mob; that it is often slow to seek the service of the best-trained gifts, and hasty to condemn the long-tried and upright public servant; — there is at least the alleviation of seeing it wake to a sense of its loss when one of its best-furnished and most faithful goes out of the contumely and fickleness of these earthly noises to where the silence is broken only by God's " Well done ! "

There is, I know, a theory which writes a new moral law of party obligations, and makes infraction of those behests one of the deadly sins. Accordin to this view, it is enough that men claim to represen the moral sentiment of the country, to enable them to communicate a sort of grace to any sinner whom they may sanctify by a nomination for office. The Church of Rome is sometimes accused of holding that a priest, though a bad man, can equally administer the sacraments; and there are those who hold that if duly named for the place, the most corrupt man is fitted to become a. high-priest in the nation's temple; there are those who hold that we elect men to keep the national conscience and are absolved from any public duty but doing as we are told. When we thus sell ourselves for nothing to the will of power, fare-well indeed to the hope of our high heritage from God! If it were so, the free spirit might well say with Lacordaire, "I am forced to leave the scene by a secret instinct of my liberty, in presence of an age which had no longer all its own. I saw that in my ideas, in my language, and in my past, I also was a liberty, and that my time was come for disappearing like the rest."

But it is not so. Christian men and women, who have to do with forming the better mind of the republic, see to it that you do your part to scatter these miasmatic vapors which threaten to stifle our best life, — and all will yet be well. Hold up afresh a higher standard of duty before others; hold to it those whom you place in power, — and test their claims by it; and that you may do so consistently, hold yourself to it. Enforce the Christian law of conscience, as personal in public as in private duty.

Honor, as the great outburst of popular respect has honored, the man who tries to do his duty.

Ah, to what wholesome lessons does the event bring us back, whose shadow is still over us! I end as I began : death teaches us much that life could never teach; — the great and solemn lesson of charity, that searching spirit of love which will find the truth in a man and hold it fast, and help it in all its strong and radiant power; the faith in the ultimate victory of the truth, which will count all else loss if we can only lose ourselves in that triumphant, much-enduring service; the trust in character, in that rocky faithfulness to one's best and deepest convictions, which

" Obeys the voice at eve
Obeyed at prime."

And this is the meaning of that wonderful outpouring of the great heart of a Commonwealth which we ourselves have seen.

" And they buried him in the city of David among the kings, because he had done good in Israel, both toward God and toward his house;" "and all Israel mourned for him, according to the word of the Lord."

Note A. Page 6. — The father of the Senator, Charles Pinckney Sumner, High Sheriff of Suffolk County, a man of stern integrity, died in April, 1839, at the same age which his distinguished son attained, — sixty-three years.

His mother, Mrs. Relief (Jacobs) Sumner, died in June, 1866, aged eighty-one years, three months, having outlived seven of her nine children, all of whom were taken away in the fulness of their promise. Mrs. Sumner was a woman of retiring simplicity of life, but of strong and heroic traits of character; and those who knew her could trace in the Senator's noblest characteristics a direct inheritance from her. The lofty and resolute sense of duty by which she was governed was strikingly illustrated by the following incident, which occurred while she was on her death-bed. A few days before she died, as a friend bent over her to receive what she supposed to be her dying message to her son, then at Washington, during the session of Congress, she caught these words from the failing lips: "Tell him his country needs him more than his mother does now." He returned, however, instantly, on receiving tidings of her fatal illness, and had the satisfaction of being with her when she died.

Mrs. Sumner's losses in her children were as follows: Matilda (twin sister with Charles), died in March, 1832, aged 21 years; Jane, died in October, 1837, aged 17 years; Mary, died in October, 1844, aged 22 years; Horace, drowned in the wreck of the ship "Elizabeth" on Long Island, July 16, 1850, on his return from abroad; Albert, lost with his family, in the wreck of the "Lyonnais," Nov. 1856; Henry, died at Orange, New Jersey, in 1856; George, died October 6, 1863, aged 46 years. Charles Sumner, Senator from Massachusetts, was born Jan. 6, 1811, and died March 11, 1874. One sister, Mrs. Julia Hastings, of San Francisco, survives him.

NOTE B. Page 6. — Probably one of the strongest influences which affected Mr. Sumner's early life was that which proceeded from Dr. Channing's "enthusiasm for Humanity." In the latest revision of his *Works*, for the edition not yet completed, he has put on record his Christian sentiments in the following, among many other similar expressions: —

"The true image of Christ is not lost. Clearer than in the venerated napkin, better than in color or marble of choicest art, it appears in each virtuous deed, in every act of self-sacrifice, in all magnanimous toil, in any recognition of human brotherhood." — *Works*, ii; 277: "War System of the Commonwealth of Nations."

"Long before philosophy deduced the law of human progress from the history of man, the gospel silently planted it in the human heart." — *Works*, ii; 99: "The Law of Human Progress."

"If any man thinks that the interest of these nations and the interest of Christianity are two separate and distinct things, I wish my soul may never enter into his secret." — *Works*, iii; 87: Motto, from Oliver Cromwell, to "Freedom National, Slavery Sectional."

And his faith in a principle characteristic of the Christian gospel is witnessed by his consistent interest in the cause of peace, — as testified alike by his earliest oration on "The True Grandeur of Nations," and by his bequest of one thousand dollars to the president and fellows of Harvard College, for an annual prize dissertation "on Universal Peace, and the Methods by which War may be Permanently Suspended."

APPENDIX.

The Funeral Services at King's Chapel and at Mount Auburn on Monday, March 16, 1874.

When it was known that the State authorities had undertaken to give a public funeral to the remains of Senator Sumner, the Wardens and Vestry of King's Chapel had at once formally placed the church at their disposal.

The following account of Monday's Services is mainly condensed from the Boston papers of March 17 : —

The members of the City Government assembled at the City Hall soon after two o'clock, and at half-past two moved in procession to King's Chapel.

At fifteen minutes before three o'clock the procession from the State House entered the church, which had been draped in mourning, and had the chancel adorned with flowers and its rail draped with American flags. His Excellency the Governor and Staff, the members of the Executive Council, Heads of Departments and Senate, members of the Society of Cincinnati * and Board of Trade, were assigned to seats on the left of the broad aisle. The pews in the left side aisle were occupied by the members of the House of Representatives. The pews at the head on the right of the broad aisle were allotted to mourners, the Vice President of the United States, the Massachusetts delegation in Congress, the Congressional Committee, and the Chaplain and Sergeant-at-Arms of the U. S. Senate. In the rear of them were seated the Judges of the Supreme Court, Judges of the United States Courts, and officers of the Army and Navy, Corporation and Overseers of Harvard College, Members of the Class of 1830, the Reverend Clergy, Massachusetts Historical Society, and Chamber of Commerce. The pall-bearers were seated at the head of the right side aisle, and below them the members of

* In pew No. 74, formerly occupied by Mr. Sumner's family.

the City Government. The Trustees of the Public Library and Art Museum and the Cambridge City Government closed the procession.

THE BURIAL SERVICE

Was according to the King's Chapel Liturgy, with special additions. Rev. Henry W. Foote officiated, and the music was selected and conducted by Mr. J. W. Tufts, the organist and director of the choir, which was composed for the occasion of twelve voices, — Mrs. Kimball, Mrs. Howard, and Mrs. West, sopranos; Mrs. Shattuck, Mrs. Sawyer, and Mrs. Barry, altos; Messrs. Collins, Fessenden, and Clark, tenors; and Messrs. Spencer. Hathorn, and Dr. Goddard, bassos.

The coffin was met at the church door by Rev. Mr. Foote, who uttered the Sentences : —

I am the Resurrection and the Life, saith the Lord : he who believeth in me, though he were dead yet shall he live ; and whosoever liveth and believeth in me shall never die.

I know that my Redeemer liveth, and that he shall stand at the latter day upon the earth. And though after my skin worms destroy this body, yet in my flesh shall I see God.

We brought nothing into this world and it is certain that we can carry nothing out. The Lord gave, and the Lord hath taken away ; blessed be the name of the Lord.

An organ prelude followed (Stradella's Largo, " O Salutaris "), and then Neumarck's Choral : —

> " To thee, O Lord, I yield my spirit,
> Who break'st in love this mortal chain.
> My life I but from thee inherit,
> And death becomes my chiefest gain.
> In thee I live, in thee I die
> Content, for thou art ever nigh."

Then followed the Burial Psalms, the choir singing the responses in Blow's setting : —

Lord, let me know my end and the number of my days ; that I may know how frail I am.

Behold, thou hast made my days as it were a span long, and mine age is even as nothing in respect to thee; and verily every man living is altogether vanity.

For man walketh in a vain shadow, and disquieteth himself in vain; he heapeth up riches and cannot tell who shall gather them.

And now, Lord, what is my hope? Truly my hope is even in thee.

I became dumb and opened not my mouth; for it was thy doing.

But take thy plague away from me; for I am consumed by the blow of thy heavy hand.

When thou with rebukes dost chasten man for sin, thou makest his beauty to consume away, like as it were a moth fretting a garment; surely every man is vanity.

Hear my prayer, O Lord, and with thine ears consider my calling; hold not thy peace at my tears.

For I am a stranger with thee, and a sojourner, as all my fathers were.

Oh spare me a little, that I may recover my strength, before I go hence, and be no more seen.

Lord, thou hast been our refuge from one generation to another.

Before the mountains were brought forth, or ever thou hadst formed the earth and the world even from everlasting to everlasting, thou art God.

Thou turnest man to destruction; and sayest, Return, ye children of men.

For a thousand years in thy sight are but as yesterday, when it is past, or a watch in the night.

Thou carriest them away as with a flood; they are even as a sleep; and fade away suddenly like the grass.

In the morning it is green, and groweth up; but in the evening it is cut down, dried up, and withered.

The days of our age are threescore years and ten; and though men be so strong that they come to fourscore years, yet is their strength then but labour and sorrow; so soon passeth it away, and we are gone.

So teach us to number our days that we may apply our hearts unto wisdom. Amen.

Then followed these Selections from Scripture : —

The burden of the valley of vision. What aileth thee now, that thou art wholly gone up to the housetops? Thou that art full of stirs, a tumultuous city.

Help. Lord! for the faithful fail from among the children of men.

All ye that are about him, bemoan him; all ye that know his name, say, how is the strong staff broken, and the beautiful rod!

To the counsellors of peace is joy. But His word was in mine heart as a burning fire shut up in my bones, and I was weary with forbearing, and I would not stay. For I heard the defaming of many. fear on every side. Report, say they, and we will report it. All my familiars watch for my halting, saying, Peradventure he will be enticed, and we shall prevail against him, and we shall take our revenge on him. . . . But, O Lord of hosts, that triest the righteous, . . . unto thee have I opened my cause.

Righteousness exalteth a nation ; but sin is a reproach to any people.

Speak unto the children of Israel . . . and proclaim liberty throughout all the land unto all the inhabitants thereof. Is not this the fast that I have chosen? to loose the bands of wickedness, to undo the heavy burdens and to let the oppressed go free, and that ye break every yoke? As free, and not using your liberty for a cloak of maliciousness, but as the servants of God.

The people that sat in darkness have seen a great light ; they that dwell in the land of the shadow of death, upon them hath the light shined.

When I went out to the gate through the city the young men saw me, and hid themselves, and the aged arose and stood up. The princes refrained talking, and laid their hands on their mouth. Because I delivered the poor that cried, and the fatherless, and him that had none to help him, the blessing of him that was ready to perish came upon me. I put on righteousness and it clothed me. I was a father to the poor ; and the cause which I knew not I searched out My glory was fresh in me ; and my bow was re-newed in my hand. Unto me men gave ear, and waited, and kept silence at my counsel.

Judge me, O Lord. for I have walked in mine integrity. I have not sat with vain persons, neither will I go in with dissemblers. I have hated the congregation of evil doers ; and will not sit with the wicked. I will wash mine hands in innocency. Gather not my soul with sinners, nor my life with bloody men: in whose hands is mischief, and their right hand is full of bribes. But as for me, I will walk in mine integrity ; redeem me and be merciful unto me.

Who shall ascend into the hill of the Lord, or who shall stand in his holy place ? He that hath clean hands and a pure heart ; who hath not lifted up his soul unto vanity nor sworn deceitfully. He shall receive the blessing from the Lord, and righteousness from the God of his salvation.

And now, behold, I am gray-headed . . . and I have walked before you from my childhood unto this day. Behold, here I am : witness against me before the Lord, and before his anointed : whose ox have I taken? or whose ass have I taken? or whom have I defrauded? or whom have I oppressed? or of whose hand have I received any bribe to blind mine eyes therewith?

But the souls of the righteous are in the hand of God, and there shall no torment touch them. There the wicked cease from troubling and the weary are at rest.

For the memorial of virtue is immortal ; because it is known with God and with men. When it is present men take example at it, and when it is gone they desire it ; it weareth a crown and triumpheth forever, having gotten the victory, striving for undefiled rewards.

Their bodies are buried in peace ; but their name liveth forevermore.

He judged the cause of the poor and needy ; then it was well with him : Was not this to know me ? saith the Lord.

What shall one then answer the messengers of the nation ? That the Lord hath founded Zion, and the poor of his people shall trust in it.

He that had received five talents came and brought other five talents, saying, Lord, thou deliverest unto me five talents ; behold, I have gained beside them five talents more. His lord said unto him, Well done, thou good and faithful servant : thou hast been faithful over a few things, I will make thee ruler over many things : enter thou into the joy of thy lord.

Finally, brethren, whatsoever things are true, whatsoever things are honest, whatsoever things are just, whatsoever things are pure, whatsoever things are lovely, whatsoever things are of good report ; if there be any virtue, and if there be any praise, think on these things.

Now is Christ risen from the dead, and become the first fruits of those who slept. For since by man came death, by man came also the resurrection of the dead.

For as in Adam all die, even so in Christ shall all be made alive. There is one glory of the sun, and another glory of the moon, and another glory of the stars ; for one star differeth from another star in glory. So also is the resurrection of the dead. It is sown in corruption, it is raised in incorruption ; it is sown in dishonor, it is raised in glory ; it is sown in weakness, it is raised in power ; it is sown a natural body, it is raised a spiritual body.

Now, this I say, brethren, that flesh and blood cannot inherit the kingdom of God ; neither doth corruption inherit incorruption. For this corruptible must put on incorruption, and this mortal must put on immortality. So when this corruptible shall have put on incorruption, and this mortal shall have put on immortality, then shall be brought to pass the saying that is written, Death is swallowed up in victory. O death, where is thy sting? O grave, where is thy victory? The sting of death is sin, and the strength of sin is the law ; but thanks be to God, who giveth us the victory through our Lord Jesus Christ.

The following anthem from Mendelssohn's St. Paul was then sung : —

Happy and blessed are they who have endured ! For though the body dies, the soul shall live forever.

At the close of the anthem, the Burial Service proceeded : —

Man who is born of a woman, hath but a short time to live, and is full of misery. He cometh up, and is cut down like a flower ; he fleeth as it were a shadow, and never continueth in one stay.

In the midst of life we are in death ; of whom may we seek for succour, but of thee, O Lord, who for our sins art justly displeased?

Yet, O Lord God most holy, O Lord most mighty, O holy and most merciful Father, deliver us not unto the bitter pains of eternal death!

Thou knowest, Lord, the secrets of our hearts; shut not thy merciful ears to our prayers; but spare us, Lord most holy, O God most mighty, O holy and merciful Father, thou most worthy Judge Eternal, suffer us not at our last hour, for any pains of death, to fall from thee.

Forasmuch as it hath pleased Almighty God to take unto himself the soul of our brother, here departed, we therefore commit his body to the ground; earth to earth, ashes to ashes, dust to dust; in sure and certain hope of the resurrection to eternal life, through our Lord Jesus Christ, when the earth and the sea shall give up their dead, and the corruptible bodies of those who sleep in Jesus shall be changed and made like unto his glorious body, according to the mighty working whereby he is able to subdue all things to himself.

Then the following Choral by Gastorius (arranged by Mr. Tufts), was sung:—

"Leave God to order all thy ways,
And hope in him, whate'er betide;
Thou 'lt find him in the evil days
Thy all-sufficient strength and guide.
Who trusts in God's unchanging love
Builds on the rock that nought can move.

"He knows when joyful hours are best,
He sends them as he sees it meet;
When thou hast borne the fiery test,
And art made free from all deceit,
He comes to thee all unaware,
And makes thee own his loving care.

"Sing, pray, and swerve not from his ways,
But do thine own part faithfully,
Trust his rich promises of grace,
So shall they be fulfilled in thee:
God never yet forsook at need
The soul that trusted him indeed."

Then followed the Collect and the special Prayer : —

Almighty God, with whom do live the spirits of those who depart hence in the Lord ; and with whom the souls of the faithful, after they are delivered from the burthen of the flesh, are in joy and felicity, we give thee hearty thanks for the good examples of all those thy servants who, having finished their course in faith, do now rest from their labours. And we beseech thee that we, with all those who are departed in the true faith of thy holy name, may have our perfect consummation and bliss in thy heavenly and everlasting glory, through Jesus Christ our Lord. Amen.

O Almighty and ever-living God, we fly to thee as our eternal refuge ; we rest ourselves upon thee, the Rock of Ages. Blessed be thy holy name for the assurance of eternal life which thou hast given us by thy beloved Son ; blessed be thy holy name for the faith which we cherish that this corruptible shall put on incorruption, and this mortal, immortality.

Let this immortal hope and the comforts of thy gracious Spirit sustain in this their bereavement the kindred and friends of our departed brother, those who are near and those who are far away. May the sorrow of the land bear up their hearts with precious consolations, and the land's sorrow be full of consecration for this great people.

Bless our beloved country, and make its rulers to rule over us for good. Teach its senators wisdom, and give to all its people a spirit of purer patriotism, inspired by thy faith and fear. May we trust not in any arm of flesh, but in the living God. Raise up wise and faithful men to guide us in the place of thy servant whom thou hast called to thy nearer service from the single-hearted and loyal discharge of his great office ; and, O God, teach us in our great loss the full lessons of his eminent and faithful life, that our gratitude may be attested by our dedication of ourselves to thy truth and thy law.

In this community, whose son he was, we thank thee for every great gift in him, of example in constancy and courage for the right, and scorn of all that was mean and low, and incorruptible integrity, — for his pleading the cause of the down-trodden and his hearing the sighing of the sorrowful, his zeal for justice and truth, for every wise word and brave and honest deed. And chiefly do we thank thee for the lofty purpose which inspired his service of his country, to give to her the best he had to give. Sanctify these great memories to us, and make them fruitful in high thinking, and faithful living to the people of this land.

Visit this mourning Commonwealth, whose heart is melted in a common sorrow, with thy Spirit of grace, to renew in us the best example of loyalty to truth and duty and thee. Purge us from all self-seeking counsels. Teach us to honor only that which is worthy of honor, and to trust only them who put their trust in thee.

Be thou, O God, our refuge and our consolation and our sure trust. The more we are brought to perceive that things seen are temporal, so much the more may we find that the things which are unseen are eternal; that thou art faithful, and that Christ is worthy, and that heaven and not earth is our home. May we embrace thy promises and be thankful; may we know that thou art God, and be still. And grant, we beseech thee, O Holy Father and Eternal Judge, that we may all live mindful of our duty and our trust, and waiting on thy will; that, when we have served thee in our generations, we may be gathered unto our fathers, having the testimony of a good conscience, and in the hope that neither death nor life, nor things present, nor things to come, will be able to separate us from the love of God, which is in Christ Jesus our Lord. Amen.

The following hymn by Montgomery was then sung by the congregation to the tune of Olmutz : —

"Servant of God, well done !
  Rest from thy loved employ ;
The battle fought, the victory won,
  Enter thy Master's joy.

"The voice at midnight came,
  He started up to hear ;
A mortal arrow pierced his frame, —
  He fell, but felt no fear.

"Tranquil amidst alarms,
  It found him on the field,
A veteran, slumbering on his arms,
  Beneath his red-cross shield.

"The pains of death are past ;
  Labor and sorrow cease ;
And, life's long warfare closed at last,
  His soul is found in peace."

The Benediction followed : —

The grace of our Lord Jesus Christ, and the love of God, and the fellowship of the Holy Ghost, be with us all evermore. Amen.

And the service was concluded with Mendelssohn's "Funeral March" and Pergolesi's "Stabat Mater."

All the way from King's Chapel to Mount Auburn the streets were lined with expectant, but hushed and reverent crowds. About a thousand colored men from all over New England awaited the funeral train in front of the State House, and attended it to Cambridge Bridge, where it was also left by the military band which had accompanied it, playing dirges.

It was nearly six o'clock when the long, imposing procession passed under the massive gateway in its winding march to the grave. It passed up Central and Walnut Avenues to Arethusa Path, where the coffin was borne, preceded by the officiating clergyman, Rev. H. W. Foote, and by the bearers, to the side of the grave. It was covered, as it had been in the church, by the most beautiful of flowers, which were buried with it.   Immediately behind the bier · came the various dignitaries who had assembled to do what honor they could to the memory of Charles Sumner, and took up their positions about the grave, his nearest friends and the Massachusetts delegation in Congress standing at the foot of the grave and a little at its left, with the committee of the Legislature by their side at its right.   At the head and just behind the clergyman stood the few surviving members of the class of 1830 in Harvard, Mr. Sumner's classmates ; while on the rising slope above and north of the grave stood the Congressional committee, the members of the Legislature, and the other invited spectators.   Behind, clustering on every hillock, pressing against the ropes on all sides, and climbing to the very summit of the hill where the tower stands, was the vast crowd of spectators, numbering many thousands, who waited in silence the last rites of sepulture.

As the body was deposited at the side of the grave a chorus of over forty male voices, selected from the Apollo Club accompanied by trombones, and led by Mr. B. J. Lang, sang the ode of

Horace, " Integer vitæ, scelerisque purus." *   While the solemn
music was rising, two daughters of Dr. Howe, the only persons
of their sex within the enclosure, stepped forward in behalf
of Mr. Sumner's absent sister, and placed upon the coffin,
already loaded with those floral designs of rarest beauty which
adorned it while the body lay in state, one a cross and the other
a wreath, which rivalled in beauty that upon which it rested.   It
was a tender tribute that moved many to tears.   Hardly had the
sounds of the singers' voices died away upon the air, when the minister, speaking so that he could be heard by all around, said :—

I heard a voice from heaven saying unto me, Write, from henceforth blessed are the dead who die in the Lord ; even so saith the
Spirit ; for they rest from their labours, and their works do follow
them.

The Lord's Prayer was afterwards said by minister and mourners, and while the remains were slowly lowered into their final rest-
ing-place, the choir sang Dr. Hedge's version (arranged by Mr.
Lang) of Luther's Choral : —

"EIN FESTE BURG IST UNSER GOTT.

" A mighty fortress is our God,
      A bulwark never failing ;
Our helper he amid the flood
      Of mortal ills prevailing ;
For still our ancient foe
Doth seek to work us woe,
His craft and power are great,
And, armed with cruel hate,
      On earth is not his equal.

" Did we in our strength confide,
      Our striving would be losing, —
Were not the right man on our side,
      The man of God's own choosing.
Dost ask who that may be ?
Christ Jesus, it is he,
Lord Sabbaoth his name,
From age to age the same,
      And he must win the battle.

---

* The Apollo Club freely accorded its aid in these services, in sympathy with
the general feeling of the community.

> " The word above all earthly powers, —
> No thanks to them, — abideth,
> The spirit and the gifts are ours
> Through Him who with us sideth.
> Let goods and kindred go,
> This mortal life also ;
> The body they may kill, —
> God's truth abideth still,
> His kingdom is forever."

As the beautiful service went on, the chorus chanting in solemn monotones the responsive " Amens," the scene was one of the most impressive which it ever falls to the lot of man to witness. The sky had taken on a subdued gray tinge, through which the light of the setting sun shone but faintly over the city of the dead. The air was silent as if the vast assembly were but breathless marble statues, and in the pauses of the service, from Boston, which lay plainly in sight towards the sea, and Cambridge and Brookline and all the neighboring cities and towns, rang slowly and faintly the vibrations of the tolling bells.

After a few moments of silence the benediction was pronounced. Then hundreds rushed forward to obtain a spray from the pile of evergreen boughs that covered the mound of earth taken from the grave. It was rapidly growing dark, and the vast crowd turned homeward, leaving the ashes to abide henceforth in peace. The spot where the body lies is in the Lot No. 2447, Arethusa Path, in the rear part of the cemetery.